The Grasshopper Laugh

Michael Bird was born in Lon
English at Oxford and taught
for several years before working in publishing.
His poetry and stories have appeared in many
magazines. He lives in Cornwall with his wife and
two young sons.

Andrew Stooke was born in London in 1959. He
studied at Camberwell School of Art and Crafts
and has exhibited widely. He lives in Dorset with
his young family, where he also teaches art.

The Grasshopper Laughs

A Faber Book of First Verse

Edited by Michael Bird
with illustrations by Andrew Stooke

ff

faber and faber
LONDON · BOSTON

for Orlando and Oscar

First published in 1995
by Faber and Faber Limited
3 Queen Square London WC1N 3AU
This paperback edition first published in 1996

Printed and bound in Great Britain by Mackays of Chatham PLC, Kent

This anthology © Michael Bird, 1996
Illustrations © Andrew Stooke, 1996

Michael Bird is hereby identified as the editor of this
work in accordance with Section 77 of the Copyright,
Designs and Patents Act 1988

A CIP record for this book
is available from the British Library

ISBN 0–571–17904–5

10 9 8 7 6 5 4 3 2 1

Contents

The cat sat asleep 3
The Little Cock 4
Dance tae yer daddy 5
Girls and boys come out to play 6
Sugarcake Bubble 7
Street Song 8
Twinkle Twinkle Firefly 9
The Lion and the Unicorn 10
Wee Willie Winkie 11
The Table and the Chair 12
Starfish 14
Minnie and Winnie 15
Good Morning,
   Mr Croco-doco-dile 16
Monkey 17
Tig 18
The Kangaroo 19
Kuk-ook's Song 20
My mother said 21
To an Isle in the Water 22
My Love for You 23
Anna Maria 24
Alas, Alack! 25
Tell a story 26
Abna Babna 27
There once was an amiable
   guinea-pig 28
Fuzzy Wuzzy 29

Pig's Song of Courtship 30
Lady and the Pig 31
The Frog 32
You spotted snakes 33
Quao 34
Others 35
Elves' Song 36
The Spikky Sparrows 37
Phinnipin 38
If you ever 40
The big ship sails 41
We have two ducks 42
The Gift Ship 43
Dandy 44
Rat-a-tat-tat 45
A cat came fiddling 46
Here we go round by
   jinga-ring 47
Fire on the Mountain 48
There was a naughty boy 49
Old Mother Goose 50
Diddle diddle dumpling 52
My Little Nut-tree 53
Calico Pie 54
The Squirrel 56
If I had a donkey 57
There was a piper 58
My Twelve Oxen 59

Move along oxen 60
Elephant 61
Tree Bear 62
Under the bamboo 63
Aiken Drum 64
Hush ye, hush ye 65
Who is the East? 66
Chamber Music 67
Green Gravel 68
This is the key 69
The Well of Life 70
Michael Finnegan 71
First Steps 72
Nuts in May 74
Rainbow Song 75
Where the bee sucks 76
Ladybird 77
Babbity Bouster Bumble
  Bee 78
The Ant had broken her
  leg 79
Skipping Rhyme 80
Humpty Dumpty 81
A Nonsense Alphabet 82
One, two, buckle my
  shoe 84
Great A, little a 86
Engine, engine 87
I had a little pony 88
The Mouse and the
  Cheese 89

Cat! 90
Travelling 92
Cow 93
Spring 94
Four and twenty tailors 9
Johnnie Crack and Flossie
  Snail 97
Meg Merrilees 98
Snail 100
Owl 101
Kookoorookoo! 102
I saw three ships 103
Weel May the Keel Row 1
Mermaid 105
The Sound of the Wind 1
Weather Rhyme 107
Don't cry! 108
Tickle Talk 109
Teapots and Quails 110
Down by the Station 112
Day mouse, night
  mouse 113
The See-Saw 114
I saw Esau 115
Jumping and Tumbling 1
All the pretty little
  horses 117
A Cradle Song 118
The Chi Chi Birds 119

When the green woods laugh with lively green,
And the grasshopper laughs in the merry scene …

William Blake

The cat sat asleep

The cat sat asleep by the side of the fire,
  The mistress snored loud as a pig;
Jack took up his fiddle by Jenny's desire,
  And struck up a bit of a jig.

The Little Cock

Peter, Peter, little cock!
Golden cock with golden comb,
Shining cock with gleaming crown,
Silken cock with silky beard,
Why are you up before the sun?
Why must you get sleepy children
Out of bed?

Traditional Russian

Dance tae yer daddy

Dance tae yer daddy,
Ma bonnie laddie,
Dance tae yer daddy, ma bonnie lamb!
An ye'll get a fishie
In a little dishie,
Ye'll get a fishie, whan the boat comes hame.

Dance tae yer daddy,
Ma bonnie laddie,
Dance tae yer daddy, ma bonnie lamb!
An ye'll get a coatie,
An a pair o' breekies,
Ye'll get a whippie, an a soople Tam.

Girls and boys come out to play

Girls and boys come out to play,
The moon doth shine as bright as day;
Leave your supper and leave your sleep,
And come to your playfellows in the street.
Come with a whoop, come with a call,
Come with a good will or not at all.
Up the ladder and down the wall,
A halfpenny roll will serve us all.
You find milk and I'll find flour,
And we'll have a pudding in half an hour.

Sugarcake Bubble

Sugarcake, Sugarcake
    Bubbling in a pot
Bubble, Bubble Sugarcake
    Bubble thick and hot

Sugarcake, Sugarcake
    Spice and coconut
Sweet and sticky
    Brown and gooey

I could eat the lot.

Grace Nichols

Street Song

One a penny poker
two a penny tongs
three a penny fire irons
HOT CROSS BUNS!

Twinkle Twinkle Firefly

Twinkle
Twinkle
Firefly
In the dark
It's you I spy

Over the river
Over the bush

Twinkle
Twinkle
Firefly
For the traveller
passing by

Over the river
Over the bush

Twinkle
Twinkle
Firefly
Lend the dark
your sparkling eye.

John Agard

The Lion and the Unicorn

The lion and the unicorn
    Were fighting for the crown;
The lion beat the unicorn
    All round the town.

Some gave them white bread,
    And some gave them brown;
Some gave them plum-cake,
    And drummed them out of town.

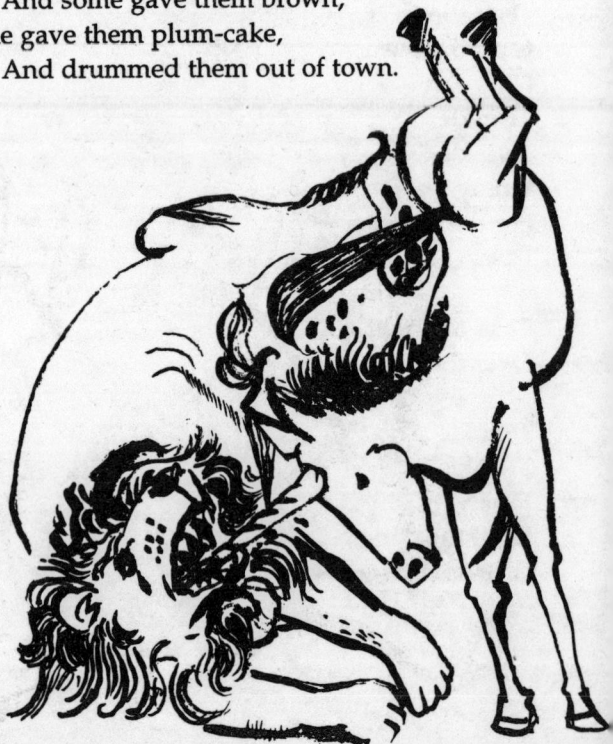

Wee Willie Winkie

Wee Willie Winkie
    Runs through the town,
Upstairs and downstairs
    In his nightgown,
Rapping at the window,
    Crying through the lock,
Are all the children in their beds?
    For now it's eight o'clock.

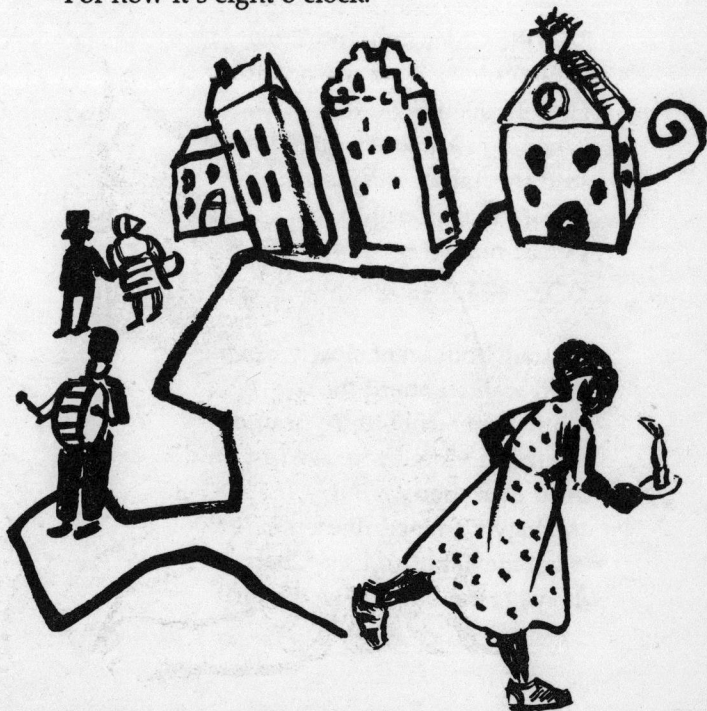

The Table and the Chair

Said the Table to the Chair,
'You can hardly be aware,
How I suffer from the heat,
And from chilblains on my feet!
If we took a little walk,
We might have a little talk!
Pray let us take the air!'
Said the Table to the Chair.

Said the Chair unto the Table,
'Now you *know* we are not able!
How foolishly you talk,
When you know we *cannot* walk!'
Said the Table with a sigh,
'It can do no harm to try,
I've as many legs as you,
Why can't we walk on two?'

So they both went slowly down,
And walked about the town
With a cheerful bumpy sound,
As they toddled round and round.
And everybody cried,
As they hastened to their side,
'See! the Table and the Chair
Have come out to take the air!'

But in going down an alley,
To a castle in a valley,
They completely lost their way,
And wandered all the day,
Till, to see them safely back,
They paid a Ducky-quack,
And a Beetle, and a Mouse,
Who took them to their house.

Then they whispered to each other,
'O delightful little brother!
What a lovely walk we've taken!
Let us dine on Beans and Bacon!'
So the Ducky, and the leetle
Browny-Mousy and the Beetle
Dined, and danced upon their heads
Till they toddled to their beds.

Edward Lear

Starfish

A Starfish stares
At stars that pour
Through depths of space
Without a shore.

She crimps her fingertips
And cries:
'If I could weep enough
Maybe
To rinse the salt
Out of my eyes
One of those dazzlers
Would be me.'

Ted Hughes

Minnie and Winnie

Minnie and Winnie
    Slept in a shell.
Sleep, little ladies!
    And they slept well.

Pink was the shell within,
    Silver without;
Sounds of the great sea
    Wander'd about.

Sleep little ladies!
    Wake not soon!
Echo on echo
    Dies to the moon.

Two bright stars
    Peep'd into the shell.
'What are they dreaming of?
    Who can tell?'

Started a green linnet
    Out of the croft;
Wake, little ladies!
    The sun is aloft!

Alfred Tennyson

Good Morning, Mr Croco-doco-dile

Good morning, Mr Croco-doco-dile,
And how are you today?
I like to see you croco-smoco-smile
In your croco-woco-way.

From the tip of your beautiful croco-toco-tail
To your croco-hoco-head
You seem to me so croco-stoco-still
As if you're croco-doco-dead.

Perhaps if I touch your croco-cloco-claw
Or your croco-snoco-snout,
Or get up close to your croco-joco-jaw
I shall very soon find out.

But suddenly I croco-soco-see
In your croco-oco-eye
A curious kind of croco-gloco-gleam,
So I just don't think I'll try.

Forgive me, Mr Croco-doco-dile
But it's time I was away.
Let's talk a little croco-woco-while
Another croco-doco-day.

Charles Causley

Monkey

Monkey see, monkey do,
Monkey get in trouble too.

Traditional Aruba

Tig

eeny meeny   figgety fig
ill doll   allymalig
blockety block   stony rock
hum bum   thrush

The Kangaroo

Old Jumpety-Bumpety-Hop-and-Go-One
Was lying asleep on his side in the sun.
This old kangaroo, he was whisking the flies
(With his long glossy tail) from his ears and his eyes.
Jumpety-Bumpety-Hop-and-Go-One
Was lying asleep on his side in the sun,
Jumpety-Bumpety-Hop!

Traditional Australian

Kuk-ook's Song

This is Kuk-ook bad boy's song.
Imakayah-hayah-ha,
Hayah-imakayah-ha!
Watch me sail away from home
In the biggest boat you've ever seen
To hunt the sweetest little girl.
I'll give her a necklace string
Of beads like bubbles in a pot,
Then when I'm ready I'll come back,
And as the grown-ups gather round
I'll show them who's boss –
Whack! Whack! Whack!
I'll marry two girls all at once.
Imakayah-hayah-ha,
Hayah-hayah-hayah-ha!
One I'll dress in spotted furs,
My other darling, she will wear
Only the soft skins of the hooded seal.

Traditional Eskimo

My mother said

My mother said that I never should
Play with the gypsies in the wood.
If I did, she would say
Naughty girl to disobey
Disobey, disobey,
Naughty girl to disobey.

I have a bonnet trimmed with blue.
Why don't you wear it? So I do.
When do you wear it? When I can,
Walking to church with my young man.

My young man has gone to France
To teach the ladies how to dance;
When he comes back he'll marry me,
Give me kisses, One-Two-Three.

Marry you! No such thing!
Yes indeed, he bought me a ring,
Bought me a biscuit, bought me a tart,
What do you think of my sweetheart!

To an Isle in the Water

Shy one, shy one,
Shy one of my heart,
She moves in the firelight
Pensively apart.

She carries in the dishes,
And lays them in a row.
To an isle in the water
With her would I go.

She carries in the candles,
And lights the curtained room,
Shy in the doorway
And shy in the gloom;

And shy as a rabbit,
Helpful and shy.
To an isle in the water
With her would I fly.

W. B. Yeats

My Love for You

I know you little, I love you lots;
My love for you would fill ten pots,
Fifteen buckets, sixteen cans,
Three teacups and four dishpans.

Anna Maria

Anna Maria she sat on the fire;
The fire was too hot, she sat on the pot;
The pot was too round, she sat on the ground;
The ground was too flat, she sat on the cat;
The cat ran away with Maria on her back.

Alas, Alack!

Ann, Ann!
    Come! quick as you can!
There's a fish that *talks*
    In the frying-pan.
Out of the fat,
    As clear as glass,
He put up his mouth
    And moaned 'Alas!'
Oh, most mournful,
    'Alas, alack!'
Then turned to his sizzling,
    And sank him back.

    Walter de la Mare

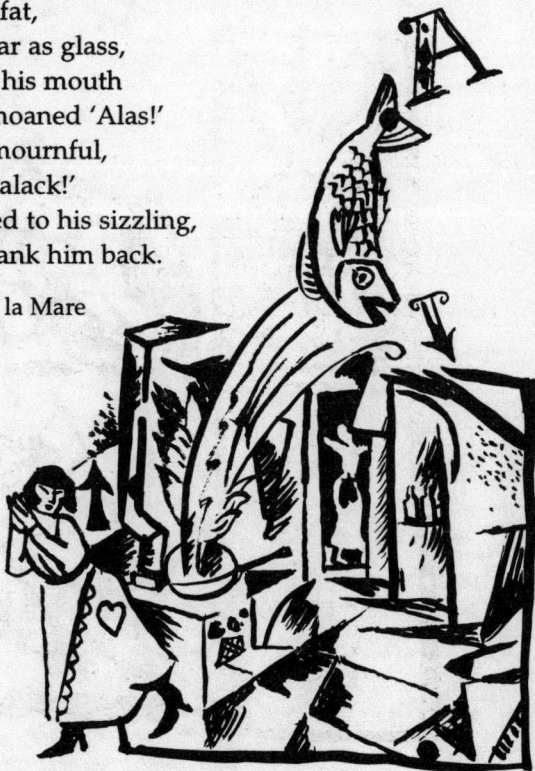

Tell a story

Tell a story,
Sing a sang;
Dae a dance,
Or oot ye gang.

Abna Babna

Abna Babna
Lady-Snee
Ocean potion
Sugar and tea
Potato roast
And English toast
out goes she.

Traditional Caribbean

There once was an amiable guinea-pig

There once was an amiable guinea-pig,
Who brushed back his hair like a periwig –

He wore a sweet tie,
As blue as the sky –

And his whiskers and buttons
Were very big.

Beatrix Potter

Fuzzy Wuzzy

Fuzzy Wuzzy was a bear.
Fuzzy Wuzzy had no hair.
So Fuzzy Wuzzy wasn't fuzzy
Was he?

Pig's Song of Courtship

Grobble Snort
Blurp Blort
Screep Uggle
Slop Snuffle
Honk Squelch
Flubber Belch
Wee Say
Wee You
Wee Love
Wee Me

John Mole

Lady and the Pig

There was a lady loved a swine,
'Honey,' quoth she,
'Pig-hog, wilt thou be mine?'
'Hough,' quoth he.

'I'll build thee a silver sty,
Honey,' quoth she,
'And in it thou shalt lie.'
'Hough,' quoth he.

'Pinned with a silver pin,
Honey,' quoth she,
'That you may go out and in.'
'Hough,' quoth he.

'Wilt thou have me now,
Honey?' quoth she,
'Speak, or my heart will break.'
'Hough,' quoth he.

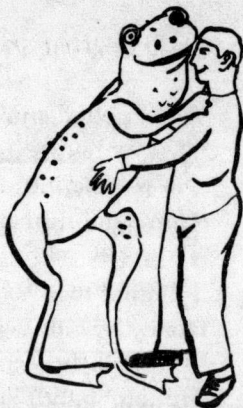

The Frog

Be kind and tender to the Frog,
    And do not call him names,
As 'Slimy skin', or 'Polly-wog',
    Or likewise 'Ugly James',
Or 'Gap-a-grin', or 'Toad-gone-wrong',
    Or 'Bill, Bandy-knees':
The Frog is justly sensitive
    To epithets like these.
No animal will more repay
    A treatment kind and fair;
At least so lonely people say
    Who keep a frog (and, by the way,
They are extremely rare).

   Hilaire Belloc

You spotted snakes

You spotted snakes with double tongue,
Thorny hedgehogs, be not seen;
Newts and blind-worms, do no wrong;
Come not near our fairy queen.
Philomel, with melody,
Sing in our sweet lullaby:
Lulla, lulla, lullaby, lulla, lulla, lullaby.
Never harm,
Nor spell, nor charm,
Come our lovely lady nigh;
So good night, with lullaby.
Weaving spiders, come not here:
Hence, you long-legged spinners, hence!
Beetles black, approach not near;
Worm, nor snail, do no offence.
Philomel, with melody,
Sing in our sweet lullaby:
Lulla, lulla, lullaby, lulla, lulla, lullaby.

William Shakespeare

Quao

Quao
is a
lizard.
He is a
wizard
at catching
flies
and other
insects
of minimal
size
who happen
to fall
in his way.
If you are
small,
then,
it would

NOT
be wise
to go
near
Quao.

Pamela Mordecai

Others

'Mother, oh mother! where shall we hide us?
Others there are in the house beside us –
Moths and mice and crooked brown spiders!'

James Reeves

Elves' Song

Buz! quoth the blue fly;
    Hum! quoth the bee:
Buz! and Hum! they cry,
    And so do we.
In his ear, in his nose,
    Thus, do you see?
He ate the dormouse:
    Else it was he.

Ben Jonson

The Spikky Sparrows

On a little piece of wood,
Mr Spikky Sparrow stood;
Mrs Sparrow sat close by,
A-making of an insect pie,
For her little children five,
In the nest and all alive,
Singing with a cheerful smile
To amuse them all the while,
    Twikky wikky wikky wee,
    Wikky bikky twikky tee,
    Spikky bikky bee!

Edward Lear

Phinniphin

The tide is in,
>The tide is in,
>>The Phinniphin
>>>Are out.

They love the sea,
>The salty sea,
>>Of this there is
>>>No doubt.

O watch them flop
>And slip and slop
>>With clumsy hop
>>>Right past

The sandy beach
>Until they reach
>>The friendly sea
>>>At last.

But when the tide,
>The shifty tide
>>Stays right outside
>>>The bar,

They can't go in
   The Phinniphin;
      The Phinniphin
         Cannot go in:
            They'd have to hop
               Too far.

Frank Collymore

If you ever

If you ever ever ever ever ever
    If you ever ever ever meet a whale,
You must never never never never never
    You must never never never touch its tail.
For if you ever ever ever ever ever
    If you ever ever ever touch its tail,
You will never never never never never
    You will never never meet another whale.

The big ship sails

The big ship sails on the alley alley oh
the alley alley oh   the alley alley oh
the big ship sails on the alley alley oh
on the last day of September

we all dip our hands in the deep blue sea
the deep blue sea   the deep blue sea
we all dip our hands in the deep blue sea
on the last day of September

The captain said this will never never do
never never do   never never do
the captain said this will never never do
on the last day of September

We have two ducks

We have two ducks. One blue, one black,
And when the blue duck goes 'Quack-quack'
our black duck quickly quack-quacks back.
The quacks Blue quacks make her quite a quacker
but Black is a quicker quacker-backer.

Dr Seuss

The Gift Ship

I saw a ship a-sailing,
    A-sailing on the sea:
And, oh! it was laden
    With pretty things for thee.

There were comfits in the cabin,
    And apples in the hold,
The sails were made of silk,
    And the masts of beaten gold.

The four and twenty sailors,
    That stood between the decks,
Were four and twenty white mice
    With chains about their necks.

The captain was a duck,
    With a packet on his back,
And when the ship began to move
    The captain said 'Quack! Quack!'

Dandy

I had a dog and his name was Dandy,
His tail was long and his legs were bandy,
His eyes were brown and his coat was sandy,
The best in the world was my dog Dandy!

Rat-a-tat-tat

Rat-a-tat-tat.
    Who is that?
Only grandma's pussy cat.
    What do you want?
A pint of milk.
    Where's your money?
In my pocket.
    Where's your pocket?
I forgot it.
    O you silly pussy cat.

A cat came fiddling

A cat came fiddling
Out of a barn
With a pair of bagpipes
Under her arm.

She could sing nothing but
'Fiddle cum fee,
The mouse has married
The bumble bee.'

Pipe cat,
Dance mouse,
We'll have a wedding
At our good house.

Here we go round by jinga-ring

Here we go round by jinga-ring,
jinga-ring, jinga-ring,
Here we go round by jinga-ring
about the merry ma tanzie.

A lump of gold to tell her name,
tell her name, tell her name,
A lump of gold to tell her name
about the merry ma tanzie.

A bottle of wine to tell his name,
tell his name, tell his name,
A bottle of wine to tell his name
about the merry ma tanzie.

Sweep the house till the bride comes home,
bride comes home, bride comes home,
Sweep the house till the bride comes home
about the merry ma tanzie.

Fire on the Mountain

Rats in the garden – catch'em Towser!
Cows in the cornfield – run boys run!
Cat's in the cream pot – stop her now, sir!
Fire on the mountain – run boys run!

There was a naughty boy

There was a naughty boy,
And a naughty boy was he.
He ran away to Scotland,
The people for to see.
 Then he found
  That the ground
  Was as hard,
  That a yard
  Was as long,
  That a song
  Was as merry,
  That a cherry
  Was as red,
  That lead
  Was as weighty,
  That four-score
  Was as eighty,
  And a door
  Was as wooden
  As in England.
 So he stood in his shoes
  And he wondered,
  He wondered,
 He stood in his shoes
  And he wondered.

John Keats

Old Mother Goose

Old Mother Goose, when
 She wanted to wander,
Would ride through the air
 On a very fine gander.

Mother Goose had a house,
 'Twas built in a wood,
Where an owl at the door
 For sentinel stood.

She had a son Jack,
 A plain-looking lad,
He was not very good,
 Nor yet very bad.

She sent him to market,
 A live goose he bought,
Here, mother, says he,
 It will not go for nought.

Jack's goose and her gander
 Grew very fond;
They'd both eat together,
 Or swim in one pond.

Jack found one morning,
 As I have been told,
His goose had laid him
 An egg of pure gold.

Diddle diddle dumpling

Diddle diddle dumpling, my son John
Went to bed with his trousers on;
One shoe off and one shoe on,
Diddle diddle dumpling my son John.

My Little Nut-tree

I had a little nut-tree,
    Nothing would it bear
But a silver nutmeg
    And a golden pear.
The King of Spain's daughter
    Came to visit me,
And all for the sake of
    My little nut tree.
I skipped over the water,
    I danced over the sea,
And all the birds in the air
    Could not catch me.

Calico Pie

Calico Pie,
The little birds fly
Down to the Calico tree,
Their wings were blue,
And they sang 'Tilly-loo!'
Till away they flew –
    And they never came back to me!
      They never came back!
      They never came back!
    They never came back to me!

Calico Jam,
The little Fish swam,
Over the syllabub sea,
He took off his hat,
To the Sole and the Sprat,
And the Willeby-wat –
    But he never came back to me!
      He never came back!
      He never came back!
    He never came back to me!

Calico Ban,
The little Mice ran,
To be ready in time for tea,
Flippity flup,
They drank it all up,
And danced in the cup,
      But they never came back to me!
          They never came back!
          They never came back!
      They never came back to me!

Calico Drum,
The Grasshoppers come,
The Butterfly, Beetle and Bee,
Over the ground,
Around and around,
With a hop and a bound –
      But they never came back!
          They never came back!
          They never came back!
      They never came back to me!

   Edward Lear

The Squirrel

The winds they did blow,
    The leaves they did wag;
Along came a beggar boy,
    And put me in his bag.

He took me up to London,
    A lady did me buy,
Put me in a silver cage,
    And hung me up on high.

With apples by the fire,
    And nuts for me to crack,
Besides a little feather bed
    To rest my little back.

If I had a donkey

If I had a donkey
And he wouldn't go,
D'you think I'd wallop him?
Oh no no!
I'd put him in the barn
And give him some corn,
The best little donkey
That ever was born.

There was a piper

There was a piper had a cow,
An he'd no hay to give her.
He took his pipes and played a tune,
Consider, old cow, consider.

The cow considered very well,
For she gave the piper a penny,
And bade him play the tune again
O'Corn rigs are Bonny.

My Twelve Oxen

With hay, with how, with hoy!
Sawest thou not my oxen, thou little pretty boy?

I have twelve oxen that be fair and brown,
and they go a-grazing down by the town.

I have twelve oxen, and they be fair and white,
and they go a-grazing down by the dyke.

I have twelve oxen, and they be fair and black,
and they go a-grazing down by the lake.

I have twelve oxen, and they be fair and red,
and they go a-grazing down by the mead.

Move along oxen

Move along oxen,
Thresh the corn faster!
You'll get the straw,
The grain's for your master.

Egyptian: from the tomb of Paheri, El-Kab, c. 1500 BC

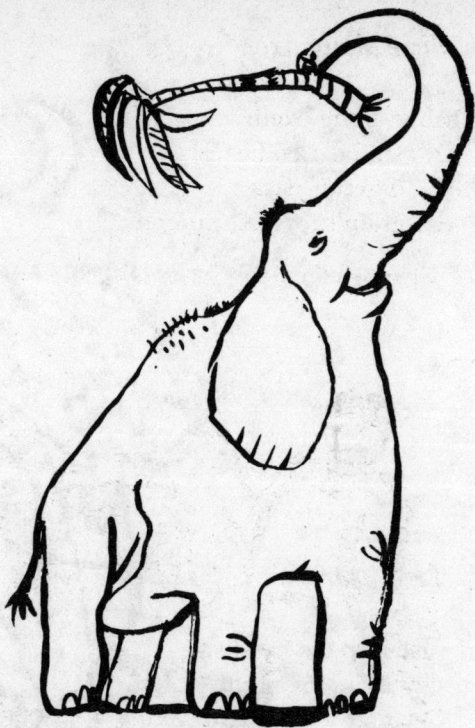

Elephant

Through the jungle the elephant goes,
Swaying his trunk to and fro,
Munching, crunching, tearing trees,
Stamping seeds, eating leaves.
His eyes are small, his feet are fat,
Hey, elephant, don't behave like that.

Traditional Indian

Tree Bear

Listen to the tree bear
Crying in the night
Crying for his mammy
In the pale moonlight.

What will his Mammy do
When she hears him cry?
She'll tuck him in a cocoa-pod
And sing a lullaby.

   Traditional Ashanti

Under the bamboo

Under the bamboo
Bamboo bamboo
Under the bamboo tree
Two live as one
One live as two
Two live as three
Under the bam
Under the boo
Under the bamboo tree.

Where the breadfruit fall
And the penguin call
And the sound is the sound of the sea
Under the bam
Under the boo
Under the bamboo tree.

T. S. Eliot

Aiken Drum

There was a man lived in the moon,
Lived in the moon, lived in the moon,
There was a man lived in the moon –
His name was Aiken Drum.

He played upon a ladle,
A ladle, a ladle,
He played upon a ladle
And his name was Aiken Drum.

Hush ye, hush ye

Hush ye, hush ye,
Little pet ye,
Hush ye, hush ye,
Dinna fret ye,
The Black Douglas
Shanna get ye.

Who is the East?

Who is the East?
The Yellow Man
Who may be Purple if He can
That carries in the Sun.

Who is the West?
The Purple Man
Who may be Yellow if He can
That lets Him out again.

Emily Dickinson

Chamber Music

Lean out of the window,
    Golden hair,
I hear you singing
    A merry air.

My book is closed;
    I read no more,
Watching the fire dance
    On the floor.

I have left my books;
    I have left my room;
For I heard you singing
    Through the gloom.

Singing and singing
    A merry air.
Lean out of the window,
    Golden hair.

James Joyce

Green Gravel

Green gravel, green gravel,
    Your grass is so green.
The fairest young maiden
    That ever was seen.

I'll wash you in new milk
    And wrap you in silk;
And write down your name
    With a gold pen and ink.

This is the key

This is the key of the kingdom:
In that kingdom there is a city.
In that city there is a town.
In that town there is a street.
In that street there is a lane.
In that lane there is a yard.
In that yard there is a house.
In that house there is a room.
In that room there is a bed.
On that bed there is a basket.
In that basket there are some flowers.
Flowers in a basket.
Basket on the bed.
Bed in the room.
Room in the house.
House in the yard.
Yard in the lane.
Lane in the street.
Street in the town.
Town in the city.
City in the kingdom.
Of the kingdom this is the key.

The Well of Life

Gently dip, but not too deep,
For fear thou make the golden beard to weep.
Fair maiden, white and red,
Comb me smooth, and stroke my head,
And thou shalt have some cockell-bread.
Gently dip, but not too deep,
For fear thou make the golden beard to weep.
Fair maiden, white and red,
Comb me smooth, and stroke my head,
And every hair a sheaf shall be,
And every sheaf a golden tree.

George Peele

Michael Finnegan

There was an old man called Michael Finnegan
He grew whiskers on his chinnegan
The wind came out and blew them in again
Poor old Michael Finnegan. Begin again …

First Steps

Stamp stamp go little feet.
Little eyes like butterflies
flap-flap-flutter.
Stamp stamp stamp stamp.
Steady, steady – yes, you're up
and walking, walking on the path.

Little feet, little feet,
where is it you're running?
– Into the forest over the moss
to get some sticks to make a fire
to warm our little cabin up
so we'll stay cosy day and night.

Little feet, little feet,
where are you going now?
– I'm running through the pinewood
to gather berries for you –
black bilberries, black bilberries
and strawberries blood-red.

Cat, cat, get off the path!
Tanechka's coming on her own two feet.
Tanechka's walking!
She won't fall,

she won't
fall. Stamp stamp stamp.

Traditional Russian

Nuts in May

Here we come gathering nuts in May,
    Nuts in May, nuts in May,
Here we come gathering nuts in May
    On a cold and frosty morning.

Who will you have for nuts in May,
    Nuts in May, nuts in May,
Who will you have for nuts in May
    On a cold and frosty morning?

Rainbow Song

Rainbow, rainbow, carry me
Across the meadows as you fly,
Not where your colours fade and die
But where they shoot down full of gold.

Traditional Russian

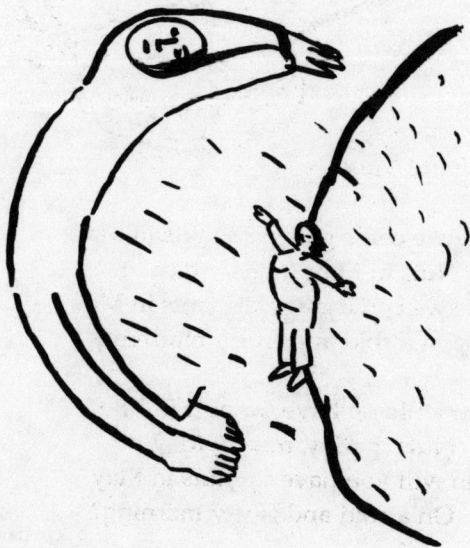

Where the bee sucks

Where the bee sucks, there suck I,
In a cowslip's bell I lie,
There I couch when owls do cry.
On the bat's back I do fly
After summer merrily.
Merrily, merrily shall I live now
Under the blossom that hangs on the bough.

William Shakespeare

Ladybird

Ladybird ladybird
fly away home
your house is on fire
and your children all gone
all except one
and that's little Ann
and she has crept under
the warming pan

Babbity Bouster Bumble Bee

Babbity Bouster Bumble Bee!
    Fill up your honey bags, bring them to me!
Humming and sighing – with lazy wing
    Where are you flying – what song do you sing?

'Who'll buy my honey-pots? Buy them, who'll buy?'
    Sweet heather honey – come weigh them and try!
– Honey-bag, honey-pot, home came she!
    Nobody buys from a big Bumble Bee!

Beatrix Potter

The Ant had broken her leg

The Ant had broken her leg,
She bound herself up with thread,
When a clock began to sing Midnight,
An Ant-Doctor ran to her bed.

The Doctor tapped on her heart,
And after, gave her this recipe:
Three times a day, a powder of sugar,
And soon you'll be better than best-can-be!

Miss Ant took the sugar-sweet powder,
Just as she had been told,
Each day she sat by the fire,
Each night she grew very cold.

She stayed in bed for four long days,
On the fifth she started to cry:
Oh! Go away you bullying pain,
I do not want to die!

So then she blew on her broken leg,
And painted her toenails red!
Next morning a happy and healthy Miss Ant
Jumped right out of her bed!

Traditional Czech, translated by Andrew Peters

Skipping Rhyme

Doctor, doctor, how's your wife?
Very bad upon my life.
Can she eat a bit of pie?
Yes she can, as well as I.

Humpty Dumpty

Humpty Dumpty ligs in t'beck
Wid a white counterpane aroon his neck,
Forty doctors and forty wrights
Will nivver put Humpty Dumpty to rights.

(Cumberland version)

from *A Nonsense Alphabet*

A
A was once an apple-pie,
Pidy
Widy
Tidy
Pidy
Nice insidy
Apple-Pie.

C
C was once a little cake,
Caky
Baky
Maky
Caky,
Taky Caky,
Little Cake!

E

E was once a little eel,
Eely
Weely
Peely
Eely
Twirly, Tweely
Little Eel!

S

S was once a little shrimp
Shrimpy
Nimpy
Flimpy
Shrimpy
Jumpy-jimpy
Little shrimp!

Edward Lear

One, two, buckle my shoe

One, two
Buckle my shoe

Three, four
Knock at the door

Five, six
Pick up sticks

Seven, eight
Lay them straight

Nine, ten
A good fat hen

Eleven, twelve
Dig and delve

Thirteen, fourteen
Maids a-courting

Fifteen, sixteen
Maids in the kitchen

Seventeen, eighteen
Maids a-waiting

Nineteen, twenty
My plate's empty

Great A, little a

Great A, little a
    Bouncing B!
The cat's in the cupboard
    And she can't see me.

Engine, engine

Engine, engine number nine
sliding down Chicago line,
when she's polished she will shine,
engine, engine number nine.

I had a little pony

I had a little pony
    His name was Dapple-grey.
I lent him to a lady,
    To ride a mile away.

She whipped him, she slashed him,
    She drove him through the mire.
I wouldn't lend my pony now,
    For all the lady's hire.

The Mouse and the Cheese

There was a wee bit moosikie,
    That lived in pantry-attay O,
But it couldna get a bit o'cheese,
    For cheekie-poussie-cattie O.
Said the moosie tae the cheesikie,
    Oh fain would I be at ye-O,
If it werena for the cruel paws
    O' cheekie-poussie-cattie O.

Cat!

Cat!
Scat!
Atter her, atter her,
Sleeky flatterer,
Spitfire chatterer,
Scatter her, scatter her
Off her mat!
Wuff!
Wuff!
Treat her rough!
Git her, git her,
Whiskery spitter!
Catch her, catch her,
Green-eyed scratcher!
Slathery
Slithery
Hisser,
Don't miss her!
Run till you're dithery,
Hithery
Thithery!
Pfitts! Pfitts!
How she spits!
Spitch! Spatch!
Can't she scratch!

Scritching the bark
Of the sycamore-tree,
She's reached her ark
And's hissing at me
Pfitts! Pfitts!
Wuff! Wuff!
Scat,
Cat!
That's
That!

Eleanor Farjeon

Travelling

One leg in front of the other,
One leg in front of the other,
    As the little dog travelled
    From London to Dover.
And when he came to a stile –
Jump! He went over.

Cow

The Cow comes home swinging
Her udder and singing:

'The dirt O the dirt
It does me no hurt.

And a good splash of muck
Is a blessing of luck.

O I splosh through the mud
But the breath of my cud

Is sweeter than silk.
O I splush through manure

But my heart stays as pure
As a pitcher of milk!'

  Ted Hughes

Spring

Sound the flute!
　　Now it's mute.
　　Birds delight
　　Day and night;
　　Nightingale
　　In the dale,
　　Lark in sky,
　　Merrily,
Merrily, merrily, to welcome in the year.

　　Little boy,
　　Full of joy;
　　Little girl,
　　Sweet and small;
　　Cock does crow,
　　So do you;
　　Merry voice,
　　Infant noise,
Merrily, merrily, to welcome in the year.

　　Little lamb,
　　Here I am;
　　Come and lick
　　My white neck;
　　Let me pull

Your soft wool;
Let me kiss
Your soft face;
Merrily, merrily, to welcome in the year.

William Blake

Four and twenty tailors

Four and twenty tailors
Went to kill a snail.
The best man amongst them
Durst not touch her tail.
She put out her horns
Like a little Kyloe cow:
Run, tailors, run!
Or she'll kill you all e'en now.

Johnnie Crack and Flossie Snail

Johnnie Crack and Flossie Snail
Kept their baby in a milking pail
Flossie Snail and Johnnie Crack
One would pull it out and one would put it back

O it's my turn now said Flossie Snail
To take the baby from the milking pail
And it's my turn now said Johnnie Crack
To smack it on the head and put it back

Johnnie Crack and Flossie Snail
Kept their baby in a milking pail
One would put it back and one would pull it out
And all it had to drink was ale and stout
For Johnnie Crack and Flossie Snail
Always used to say that stout and ale
Was *good* for a baby in a milking pail

Dylan Thomas

Meg Merrilees

Old Meg she was a gipsy,
And lived upon the moors,
Her bed it was the brown heath turf,
Her house was out of doors.

Her apples were swart blackberries,
Her currants pods o' broom,
Her wine was dew of the wild white rose,
Her book a churchyard tomb.

Her brothers were the craggy hills,
Her sisters larchen trees –
Alone with her great family
She lived as she did please.

No breakfast had she many a morn,
No dinner many a noon,
And 'stead of supper she would stare
Full hard against the moon.

But every morn of woodbine fresh
She made her garlanding,
And every night the dark glen yew
She wove, and she would sing.

And with her fingers, old and brown
She plaited mats o' rushes,
And gave them to the cottagers
She met among the bushes.

John Keats

Snail

Snail upon the wall,
Have you got at all
Anything to tell
About your shell?

Only this, my child –
When the wind is wild,
Or when the sun is hot,
It's all I've got.

John Drinkwater

Owl

A wise old owl lived in an oak;
    The more he saw the less he spoke.
The less he spoke the more he heard:
    Why can't we all be like that wise old bird?

Kookoorookoo!

'Kookoorookoo! kookoorookoo!'
    Crows the cock before the morn;
'Kikirikee! kikirikee!'
    Roses in the east are born.

'Kookoorookoo! kookoorookoo!'
    Early birds begin their singing;
'Kikirikee! kikirikee!'
    The day, the day, the day is springing.

Christina Rossetti

I saw three ships

I saw three ships come sailing by,
   Come sailing by, come sailing by;
I saw three ships come sailing by,
   On New Year's Day in the morning.

And what do you think was in them then,
   Was in them then, was in them then?
And what do you think was in them then,
   On New Year's Day in the morning?

Three pretty girls were in them then,
   Were in them then, were in them then;
Three pretty girls were in them then,
   On New Year's Day in the morning.

And one could whistle, and one could sing,
   And one could play on the violin –
Such joy there was at my wedding,
   On New Year's Day in the morning.

Weel May the Keel Row

As I cam doon the Sandgate,
The Sandgate, the Sandgate,
As I cam doon the Sandgate,
I heard a lassie sing.

'O, weel may the keel row,
The keel row, the keel row,
O, weel may the keel row,
The ship ma laddie's in.

'He wears a blue bunnet,
Blue bunnet, blue bunnet;
He wears a blue bunnet,
An a dimple in his chin.

'An weel may the keel row,
The keel row, the keel row;
An weel may the keel row,
The ship ma laddie's in.'

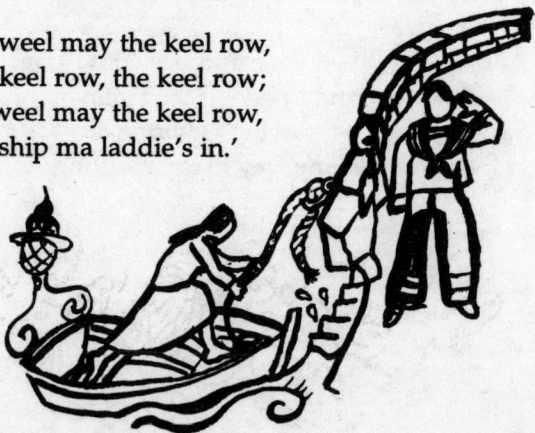

Mermaid

Call her a fish,
Call her a girl.
Call her a pearl

Of an oyster fresh
On its pearly dish

That the whole sea sips
With gurgly slurps
And sloppy lips.

Ted Hughes

The Sound of the Wind

The wind has such a rainy sound
    Moaning through the town,
The sea has such a windy sound –
    Will the ships go down?

The apples in the orchard
    Tumble from their tree –
Oh will the ships go down, go down,
    In the windy sea?

Christina Rossetti

Weather Rhyme

Rain rain go to Spain
Come again another day
When I brew and when I bake
I'll give you a figgy cake

Don't cry!

Please don't please don't please don't cry,
and I'll buy you a gingerbread man.

Please don't howl don't howl don't howl,
and I'll buy you another one.

Don't roar don't roar don't roar and shake,
and I'll buy you a honey cake!

Traditional Russian

Tickle Talk

Tae titly
little fitty
shin sharpy
knee knapy
hinchie pinchy
wymie bulgy
breast berry
chin cherry
moo merry
nose nappy
ee winky
broo brinky
ower the croun
and awa wi it

Brow bender
eye peeper
nose deeper
mouth eater
chin chopper
knock at the door
ring the bell
lift up the latch
walk in
take a chair
sit by there
how dyou do this morning?

from *Teapots and Quails*

Teapots and Quails,
Snuffers and snails,
Set him a sailing
and see how he sails!

Mitres and beams,
Thimbles and Creams,
Set him a screaming
and hark! how he screams!

Ribands and pigs,
Helmets and Figs,
Set him a jigging
and see how he jigs!

Tadpoles and Tops,
Teacups and Mops,
Set him a hopping
and see how he hops!

Lobsters and owls,
Scissors and fowls,
Set him a howling
and hark how he howls!

Eagles and pears,
Slippers and Bears,
Set him a staring
and see how he stares!

Sofas and bees,
Camels and Keys,
Set him a sneezing
and see how he'll sneeze!

Thistles and Moles,
Crumpets and Soles,
Set it a rolling
and see how it rolls!

Hurdles and Mumps,
Poodles and pumps,
Set it a jumping
and see how it jumps!

Pancakes and Fins,
Roses and Pins,
Set him a grinning
and see how he grins!

   Edward Lear

Down by the station

Down by the station early in the morning,
See the little puffer bellies all in a row.
See the engine driver pull the little throttle;
Puff, puff! Toot! Toot! Off we go.

Day mouse, night mouse

DAY MOUSE:
Tsiku icha, tsiku icha icha
Dawn, day; dawn, day day
That Tsambe mouse is eating everything!

NIGHT MOUSE:
Tsiku bakala, tsiku bakala
Stay a little, stay a little
Night, while I feed with you!

Traditional African: Nyanja people

The See-Saw

Two little mice were playing a game
– Thingummy-jig and Whatzisname –
'You're too little and I'm too big,'
Said Whatzisname to Thingummy-jig.

'You're too tiny but *I* am too tall!'
'*I*'m enormous but *you* are small!'
Up and down – 'Why we're just the same!'
Said Thingummy-jig to Whatzisname.

Beatrix Potter

I saw Esau

I saw Esau sawing wood,
And Esau saw I saw him;
Though Esau saw I saw him saw,
Still Esau went on sawing.

Jumping and Tumbling

In jumping and tumbling
    We spend the whole day,
Till night by arriving
    Has finished our play.

What then? One and all,
    There's no more to be said,
As we tumbled all day,
    So we tumble to bed.

All the Pretty Little Horses

Hush-a-bye, don't you cry,
Go to sleepy little baby.
When you wake
You shall have
All the pretty little horses.
Blacks and bays,
Dapples and greys,
Coach and six white horses.

Hush-a-bye, don't you cry,
Go to sleepy little baby.
When you wake
You shall have cake
And all the pretty little horses.

A Cradle Song

Sweet dreams, form a shade
O'er my lovely infant's head;
Sweet dreams of pleasant streams
By happy, silent, moony beams.

Sweet sleep, with soft down
Weave thy brows an infant crown.
Sweet sleep, Angel mild,
Hover o'er my happy child.

Sweet smiles, in the night
Hover over my delight;
Sweet smiles, Mother's smiles,
All the livelong night beguiles.

William Blake

The Chi Chi Birds

All the chi chi birds they sing 'til dawn.
When the daylight comes all the birds are gone.
Chi, chi, chi, chi, chi, chi, what a pretty song.
That is what the birds are singing all night long.

Bam chi chi bam, they sing-a this song,
Bam chi chi bam, sing all the night long.
Bam chi chi bam, then just before day,
Bam chi chi bam, they fly away.

Traditional

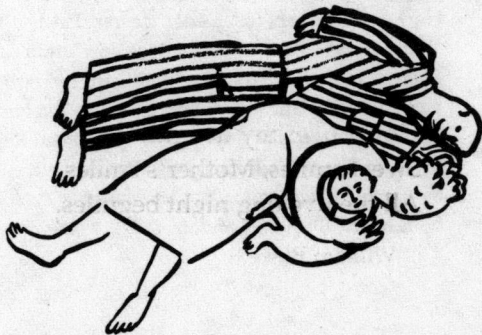

Acknowledgements

I would like to thank Jane Feaver at Faber and Faber for her enthusiasm and guidance; Daphne West, for finding the Russian rhymes in this anthology and providing prose versions from which I have worked into verse; and my wife Felicity, for the surest sense of which poems passed the crucial bedtime read-aloud test.   M.B.

Thanks must also go to the following authors, publishers and others for permission to include the poems listed here: the Estate of James Joyce for 'Chamber Music: V' ('Lean out of the window'); David Higham Associates for 'Johnny Crack and Flossie Snail' (from *Under Milk Wood*) by Dylan Thomas and 'Cat' by Eleanor Farjeon; Faber and Faber Ltd for 'Cow' , 'Mermaid' and 'Starfish' by Ted Hughes, 'Under the Bamboo' (from 'Sweeney Agonistes') by T. S. Eliot from *Collected Poems 1909–1962*, 'The Big Ship Sails', 'Tig', 'Ladybird', 'Tickle Talk' from *The Faber Book of Vernacular Verse*, edited by Tom Paulin (London, 1990), 'Engine, engine' from *The Faber Book of Nursery Verse*, edited by Barbara Ireson (London, 1958); the Literary Trustees of Walter de la Mare and The Society of Authors for 'Alas, Alack!' by Walter de la Mare from *The Complete Poems of Walter de la Mare* (London, 1969); Chambers Harrap Publishers for 'Dance tae yer daddy', 'Hush ye, hush ye', 'Tell a story', 'Weel May the Keel Row' from *Scottish Nursery Rhymes*, edited by Norah and William Montgomerie (Edinburgh, 1985); Oxford University Press for 'My Twelve Oxen' (adapted by the editor) from *The Oxford Book of Medieval English Verse*, edited by Celia Sisam (Oxford, 1970), 'This is the Key', 'The Well of Life' by George Peele, from *The Oxford Book of Poetry for Children*, edited by Edward Blishen (London, 1963), 'I saw three ships', 'Owl',

'Great A, little a', 'Old Mother Goose' from *Lavender's Blue: A Book of Nursery Rhymes*, edited by Kathleen Lines, (Oxford, 1954), 'Jumping and Tumbling' from *The Oxford Book of Children's Verse*, edited by Iona and Peter Opie (Oxford, 1973); John Agard, c/o Caroline Shelden Agency, for 'Twinkle Twinkle Firefly' from *No Hickory, No Dickory, No Dock* (Puffin, 1991); Penguin Books Ltd for 'Sugarcake Bubble' by Grace Nichols and 'Abna Babna' from *No Hickory, No Dickory, No Dock* (Puffin, 1991), for 'My Mother Said', 'There Was a Lady', 'Here we go round by jinga-ring' and 'Humpty Dumpty' from *The Puffin Book of Nursery Rhymes*, edited by Iona and Peter Opie, and to Charles Causley for 'Good Morning, Mr Croco-doco-dile' from *Early in the Morning* (Viking Kestrel, 1986); to Peters Fraser & Dunlop Group Ltd for Hilaire Belloc's 'The Frog' from *Complete Verse*; the Estate of James Reeves for 'Other', copyright James Reeves from *Complete Poems for Children* (Heinemann); Frederick Warne for 'There Once was an Amiable Guinea-Pig', 'Babbity Bouster Bumble Bee' and 'The See-Saw' by Beatrix Potter; Mrs Frank Collymore for 'Phinniphin' by Frank Collymore; Pamela Mordecai for 'Quao'; Andrew Peters for his version of 'The Ant had Broken her Leg'; John Mole for 'Pig's Song of Courtship' from *The Mad Parrot's Countdown* (Peterloo Poets), copyright John Mole, 1990; the publishers and the Trustees of Amherst College for 'Who is the East?' from *The Poems of Emily Dickinson*, edited by Thomas H. Johnson, Cambridge, Mass.: The Belknap Press of Harvard University Press, copyright 1951, 1955, 1979, 1983 by the President and Fellows of Harvard College. The original version of 'Kuk-ook's Song' comes from *The Sky Clears: Poetry of the American Indians* by A. Grove Day and is used by permission of the University of Nebraska Press; this version has been adapted by Michael Bird, who has also provided his own version of 'Move Along Oxen'.